Jesus The Light of The World

Special Thanks

These studies are the work of the Holy Spirit, who provided guidance, wisdom, instruction, and inspiration. Special thanks to Elder Alfonza Watson for his patience, time, love, and devotion to the Lord. I am so grateful for the support and love of my family and friends. I want to acknowledge the hard work of my granddaughter Katherine Jones who went through each Bible study and notes to ensure they were written for young people ages 12 and older. Finally, I cannot claim what is not mine; to the Holy Spirit, I say thank you for trusting me with God's Word that others may find God. This is your work—I take no credit for any of your work.

The Word of God Foundational Bible Study revised edition is dedicated to the work of Prison Ministry worldwide. I pray that the Holy Spirit works through you to share the blessings of salvation to incarcerated men, women, youth, and their families.

Let your light so shine before men, that they may see your good works, and glorify your Father which is in heaven. Matthew 5:16

Planting the seeds for the Harvest of the Lord

Then saith he unto his disciples, The harvest truly is plenteous, but the laborers are few;   Pray ye therefore the Lord of the harvest, that he will send forth laborers into his harvest. Matthew 9:37-38

WELCOME to *The Word of God Foundational Bible Study.* This Bible study is designed to introduce you to Jesus Christ and build your relationship with Christ. Scripture used in this study is taken from the New King James Version of the Bible (and a few from The Amplified Bible where indicated).

Through Bible study and the opening of my heart to the Holy Spirit, We are studying the Bible first from a desire to know God

It is by faith, trusting, and accepting God's word we learn of Jesus Christ, His teaching, and why we need Him in our lives.

I am come a light into the world, that whosoever believeth on me should not abide in darkness" (John 12:46)

"Then spake Jesus again unto them, saying, I am the light of the world: he that followeth me shall not walk in darkness, but shall have the light of life" (8:12). As you go through these studies, I encourage you to invite Jesus into your heart.

The Purpose of Bible Study

GOD PROVIDES SIMPLE but clear application for us in the discernment of truth. Second Timothy 2:15: "Study to shew thyself approved unto God, a workman that needeth not to be ashamed, rightly dividing the word of truth." God provides doctrine based on his infallible and perfect Word. He reproves us as needed, corrects us, and gives us instruction in every situation we will encounter in life. Second Timothy 3:15-17: "And that from a child thou hast known the Holy Scriptures, which are able to make thee wise unto salvation through faith which is in Christ Jesus. All scripture is given by inspiration of God, and is profitable for doctrine, for reproof, for correction, for instruction in righteousness: That the man of God may be perfect, thoroughly furnished unto all good works." **We must see Christ in each of our studies. Prophecies are open-ended to establish validity.**

We all have questions, but God does not leave us wondering. He gives answers in his Word. Psalms 119:41-42: "Let thy mercies come also unto me, O LORD, even thy salvation, according to thy word. So shall I have wherewith to answer him that reproacheth me: for I trust in thy word."

What is life without joy? True joy comes from God. Psalms 119:103: "How sweet are thy words unto my taste! Yea, sweeter than honey to my mouth!"

Here are a few recommended study tips to enhance your time in Scripture and draw you closer to Christ:

Always start your study with prayer.
Ask the Holy Spirit to guide and teach you as you study.

Approach each study with an open mind, allowing the Holy Spirit to work in you.
Write down words or phrases that are unfamiliar or unclear. Takes notes (look up keywords).
Ask the following questions:

> Who is speaking in the passage?
> Who is the passage speaking to?
> What is the context of the passage?
> What is the situation around the passage?
> Where is the setting of the passage?
> When is the setting of the passage?

> Review what you have learned.
> Apply what you have learned.

Elements of Preparation for Good Bible Study

GOD'S INSPIRED WORD. Second Peter 1:20-21: "Knowing this first that no prophecy of the scripture is of any private interpretation. For the prophecy came not in old time by the will of man: but holy men of God spake as they were moved by the Holy Ghost."

Personal--**Psalms 119:16**: "I will <u>delight</u> myself in thy statutes: I will not forget thy word."

Prayer--- **Psalms 119:18**: To open eyes to behold wondrous things. "<u>Open</u> thou mine eyes, that I may behold wondrous things out of thy law."

Teachable spirit. **Psalms 119:33**: "<u>Teach</u> me, O LORD, the way of thy statutes; and I shall keep it unto the end."

Apply daily--Sanctify yourself and apply God's Word. **Psalms 119:101**: "I have refrained my feet from every evil way, that I might <u>keep</u> thy word."

Four Simple Steps to Ensure Bible Study Is Successful

1. Study **systematically**. In other words, focus on one topic at a time. This provides purpose, clarity, and a deeper relationship with God on your journey.

2. Study **thoroughly**. For example, if you are studying the concept of *Grace*, you must read and study every reference to the word in order to acquire a holistic view.

3. Study **deeply.** Examine what God's perfect Word is saying by using different translations. This will make the Bible clearer.

4. Study **formally**. Take notes to help you reference what you have learned. Your notes will assist you as you continue to study God's Word.

Table of Contents

LESSON 1 The Holy Bible: True or False?

Purpose:　　To understand that the Bible is God's Word

Objectives: To understanding why God gave us the Bible

To learn about Jesus

1. "In the beginning we find the following out about God and the Word (Bible) **John 1:1**

    a. ____

    b. ____

    c. ____

This means that the______________________ and God are the same.

2. What are the four things Scripture is given for?
2 Timothy 3:16

    a. ____

    b. ____

    c. ________________________________

    d.________________________________

3. When does the Bible say is the right time a person
   should begin learning the scriptures? **2 Timothy 3:15**

____

____

____

4. What does the Bible say about prophecy in Scripture**?**
2 Peter 1:20

____

____

____

5. How did holy men write the Scriptures? **2 Peter 1:21**

____

____

____

6. What is the purpose of Scripture? **Romans 15:4**

   a. _______________________________________

   b. _______________________________________

> **Note:** The Bible is God's written Word to humanity. It serves as a way of connecting the human race with God through His character, purpose, promises, wisdom, guidance, and answers. **John 14:6** says, "Jesus saith unto him, I am the way, the truth, and the life: no man cometh unto the Father, but by me."

7. Why should we study the Bible? **2 Timothy 2:15**

   ____

   ____

8. How should we study the Bible? **Isaiah28:10**

   a. ____

   b ____

9. "Thy ________________ is a lamp unto my feet, and a _

________________________ unto my path **Psalms 119:105**.

10. "Then Jesus spoke to them again, saying

____

____

____

John 8:12

11. He answered and said, 'It is written, _

____ shall not live by bread

alone, but by every ______________ that proceedeth out of

the mouth of ____________________ **Matthew 4:4**

Summary

1. God and the Word are the Same **John 1:1**

2. God gave us the Bible for doctrine, for reproof, for correction, for instruction in righteousness **2 Timothy 3:15**

3. Holy men wrote the Bible **2 Peter 1:21**

4. Jesus is the light of the world **John 8:12**

5. Man can't leave on bread alone He needs Jesus **Matthew 4:4**

LESSON 2 Why Study the Bible?

Purpose: To know why we should study the Bible

Objectives: To understand God's character

To introduce Jesus to you and me

.

1. What is the purpose of Bible study?

____

____

____

Romans 15:4

2. ______________________to show thyself ________________

unto God, a workman that needeth not to be ashamed,

rightly dividing the word of truth" **2 Timothy 2:15**.

3. "According to God, what are the 2 things we should
    not do to scriptures?

a. ____

b ____
   Deuteronomy 4:2

4. "Teach me Your ____________________-, O Lord; I

will walk in Your ____________________; [a] Unite

my heart to fear Your name. **Psalms 86:11**

Walk means to follow in Jesus footsteps; God's word is truth.

5. What is the character of God? **Psalms 86:15**

A. ____

B. ____

6. Who should teach all things? **John 14:26**

____

7. By allowing the Holy Spirit control of my Bible

Study, what two things will happen? **John 16:13**

____

____

____

> **Note:** We must approach God's Word with an open
> mind. This means seeking God's Holy Spirit to guide us
> and be as He is and not as we would like Him to be.

8. What four things can we gain from Bible study? **Job 12:13**

A. ____

B. ____

C. ____

B. ____

Note: Study of God's word will:
(a) Introduce us to God the Father, the Son of
Man Jesus Christ, and the Holy Spirit.
(b) It will teach you about God's character.
(c) It will provide answers to unanswered
questions, and it will draw you nearer to Jesus.

9. What did Jesus say is necessary for man to fully live? "But

He answered and said, It is written, **Man** shall not live by _

______________alone, but by every ________________that

proceedeth out of the ___________________of God."
Matthew4: 4

10. Spending time in Bible study, we can learn the facts

about creation. "In the _______________________________God _

________________________the heaven and the earth." **Genesis.
1:1**

11. Who is love? **John 4:7**

____

____

____

12. "What did God do because He loves us so much? **John
    3:16**

____

____

____

13. "Why did God send His son? **John 3:16**

____

____

13. Through Bible study, we learn about the power of God's

Word. For He ____________________, and it was done; He

__________________________, and it stood fast.
   Psalms 33:9

14. He who ___________ is of the _______________ for

the devil has sinned from the beginning. For this purpose the

Son of God was manifested, that He might destroy the works of

the devil. **1 John 3:8**

Summary

1. Do not change God's word; **Deuteronomy 4:2**

2. Let the Holy Spirit control of your Bible Study;
   John 16:13

3. Through Bible study we learn about creation.
   Genesis. 1:1

4. God send His son to save us; **John 3:16**

5. Son of God will destroy the works of the devil.
   1 John 3:8

Introducing the Holy Spirit

The Holy Spirit is mentioned more than a hundred times in Scripture: How important is He? He is infinitely important because the Holy Spirit is God speaking to you! Will you take the time to meet the Holy Spirit?

MANY OF US may have very basic questions about this mysterious person known as the Holy Spirit (or to some, the Holy Ghost). We may find ourselves searching the scriptures, questioning our family and friends, and consulting church leaders. Through prayer, Bible study, faith, and a dependence on our personal relationship with God, we can find answers. This study will provide many answers and provide a foundation for a deeper understanding of who the Holy Spirit is, what He does, and why we need Him in our lives.

LESSON 3 The Holy Spirit

Purpose: To understand who the Holy Spirit is

Objectives: To understand the importance of the Holy Spirit

To understand the work of the Holy Spirit

To understand the symbols of the Holy Spirit

To understand that Holy Spirit is a person.

1. Has the Holy Spirit existed from the very beginning? **Genesis1:2**

____

2. What did the Holy Spirit do when the earth was dark at

creation? **Genesis 1:2**

____

____

____

3. Why did God send His son? **John 3:16**

____

____

____

2. "You send forth Your _____________________ they are

created; And You renew the face of the earth.

Psalms104:30

3. "The _______________of God hath _____________me, and

the breath of the Almighty hath given me life" **Job 33:4**.

4. Go therefore and make disciples of all the nations,

baptizing them in the name of the Father and of the Son and of

the_____________________________________ , **Matthew. 28:19**.

5. The grace of the Lord Jesus Christ, and the

love of God, and the communion of the _______________

________________ be with you all. Amen.
   2 Corinthians 13:14

6. But Peter said, "Ananias, why has Satan filled your heart

to lie to the ___________________________ and keep back

part of the price of the land for yourself? **Acts 5:3**

7. What 2 things will the Holy Spirit do for us? **John 14:26**

____

____

____

____

8. **FILL IN THE BLANKS IN THE CHART BELOW**

The Holy Spirit reveals the ___________	**Matthew 11:27**
The Holy Spirit Shall ___________	**John 14:26**
The Holy Spirit___________in us	**1 Corinthians 3:16**
9. Is the Holy Spirit a person? Yes ____ No ______	
The Holy Spirit reveals the ___________	**1 Corinthians 12:3**
The Holy Spirit has a ___________	**Romans 8:27**
The Holy Spirit has a ___________	**1 Corinthians 12:11**
The Holy Spirit has ___________	**1 Corinthians 2:11**
The Holy Spirit has ___________	**Romans 15:30**
The Holy Spirit is ___________	**Psalms. 143:10**

10. Fill in the blank with the correct symbol of the Holy Spirit:

    a. Genesis 2:7 _______________________________

    b. Psalms 51:11 _____________________________

    c. Leviticus 8:10-12 _________________________

    d. Matthew 3:16 _____________________________

    e. Ephesians 1:13 ___________________________

    f. Exodus 3:2 _______________________________

    g. John 7:37-39 _____________________________

Summary

1. The Holy Spirit has always existed **Genesis1:2**

2. The Holy Spirit reveals Jesus **Matthew 11:27**

3. The Holy Spirit lives in us **1 Corinthians 3:16**

4. The Holy Spirit has love **Romans 15:30**

5. The Holy Spirit brings all things to your remembrance
John 14:26

LESSON 4 Basic Instructions Before Leaving Earth (B.I.B.L.E.)

Purpose: To understand the purpose of Scripture

Objectives: To understand how Scripture impacts us

To understand scripture is filled with love

1. Why did God give us the Bible **2 Timothy 3:16**

A ____

B ____

C ____

D ____

2. What 2 things happen to us when we study God's word?
2 Timothy 3:17

A ____

B ____

3. The Lord is good to _____________, And His tender mercies
are over all His works. **Psalms 145:9**

Note: Knowledge comes through understanding.
What good is knowledge if you do not understand
and apply it daily? God's Word requires reading
for understanding and application of that
understanding in our daily lives. Once we have
studied precept upon precept, it is time to live
those precepts. Then shall the purpose of the
Scripture be fully understood, and the blessings of
God shall be a declaration of Jesus Christ.

---

4. What warning does God give us about adding to the Bible?
    Revelation 22:18-19

____

____

____

5. What warning does God give us about taking a thing away from the Bible? (**Revelation 22:18-19**

____

____

____

____

> **Note:** God's word is perfect; it tells us who God is, and it's filled with love, hope, and blessings. God is one who knows all things and has given us written instructions about everything we need to know in His Bible. This is why we don't need to add or take away anything from God's Word.

6. "How does God love me? **Jeremiah 31:3**

____

____

____

7. What has God promised me? (**1 John 2:25**.

____

____

____

8. What three promises listed in **John 14:2-3** does the Lord make to His followers?

A ____

B ____

C ____

9. What does Paul say we are to put on daily? **Ephesians 6:11**

____

10. What is the sword of the Christian? **Ephesians 6:17**

____

12. What are we to do without ceasing? 1 **Thessalonians 5:17**

____

13. Let your _______________ therefore be _______________

to the Lord our God, to walk in His statutes and keep His

_______________________ as at this day. **1 Kings 8:61**

14. Read **Hebrews 4:12**, and list the four things we should know

about the Word of God.

A ____

B ____

C ____

D ____

Summary

1. There are benefits to studying God's word?
   2 Timothy 3:17

2. God loves me? **Jeremiah 31:3**

3. God has promised for me? **1 John 2:25, John 14:2-3**

4. We are to pray without ceasing? **1 Thessalonians5:17**

5. God warns us not to add or take away from the Bible?
   Revelation 22:18-19

LESSON 5   What Is Sin?

Purpose: To understand what sin is

Objectives: To understanding the result of sin

To understand Jesus is the answer to sin

1. "What is sin **1 John 3:4**.

____

____

____

2. According to **Revelation 12:9**, who is the great Serpent and what will happen to him?

a. The great Serpent is ____________________

b. He was ____________________________________

3. How was Lucifer created? **Ezekiel 28:15**.

____

4. How do we Know sin **Romans 3:20**.

____

5. Therefore, to him who ___________ to do good and

Does not do it, to him it is __________ . **James 4:17**

6. How many have sinned? **Romans 3:23**.

____

7. The devising of ____________________- is sin,

And the scoffer is an abomination to men. **Proverbs 24:9**

Sin separates us from God. Think of it this way: light and darkness cannot coincide in the same place at the same time. There is either darkness or light, but never both together. Without God we live in darkness. **John 12:46** says "I am come a light into the world, that whosoever believeth on me should not abide in darkness." **Act 26:18** "To open their eyes, and to turn them from darkness to light, and from the power of Satan unto God, that they may receive forgiveness of sins, and inheritance among them which are sanctified by faith that is in me."

8. "Righteousness exalteth a nation: but _________ is a reproach

to any people" **Proverbs. 14:34**

9. Therefore, just as through one man _____________ entered the world,

and death through _____________, and thus death spread to all men,

because all _______________ **Romans. 5:12**

10. For thus says the Lord: 'Your affliction is

___________________________, Your wound is severe.

Jeriamiah.30:12

11. But if we walk in the _______________ as He is in the

______________, we have fellowship with one another, and the blood
   of Jesus Christ His Son cleanses us from all __________________.
   1 John 1:7

12. Then Jesus spoke to them again, saying, "I am the

_______________ of the world. He who follows Me shall not walk

in darkness, but have the _____________of life. **John 8:12**

13. For God hath not appointed us to wrath, but to obtain

_______________________________by our Lord ___________________________
1 Thessalonians 5:9

Summary

1. There are benefits to studying God's word? **2 Timothy 3:17**

2. God loves me! **Jeremiah 31:3**

3. God has promised me eternal life. **1 John 2:25, John 14:2-3**

4. We are to pray without ceasing! **1 Thessalonians 5:17**

5. God warns us not to add or take away from the Bible! **Revelation 22:18-19**

LESSON 6   God's Ten Commandments

Purpose: To develop a knowledge of the 10 Commandments

Objectives: To understand why God gave the 10 Commandments

To see God's character in the 10 Commandments

1. And when He had made an end of speaking with him on

Mount Sinai, He gave Moses two _________________ of the

Testimony, _________________ of stone, written with the

finger of God. **Exodus 31:18**

2. He took the _____________________ and put it into

the ark, inserted the poles through the rings of the ark, and

put the _______________________ on top of the ark

Exodus 40:20

> **Note:** The mercy seat was a lid or covering located in the most Holy place. It represented the presence of God. **Exodus 25:21-22** You shall put the mercy seat on top of the ark, and in the ark you shall put the Testimony that I will give you. 22 And there I will meet with you, and I will speak with you from above the mercy seat, from between the two cherubim which are on the ark of the Testimony, about everything which I will give you in commandment to the children of Israel.

3. The law of the Lord is _________________converting the soul;

The testimony of the Lord is _______________, making wise the

Simple; 8 The statutes of the Lord are _____________, rejoicing

the heart; The commandment of the Lord is ___________,

enlightening the eyes;" **Psalms 19:7-8**

4. "The works of his hands are verity and judgment; and his

__________________are sure. They stand fast

__________________, and are done in truth and uprightness"
Psalms 111:7-8

5. "Wherefore the law is _____, and the commandment _____,

And ____________________, and ____________________"
Romans 7:12

6. "I am clean without ________, I am _________; neither

there ______________________in me" **Job 33:9**

7. "Whosoever committeth sin transgresseth also the law: for sin is

the transgression of the law. Sin is the ____________________of

the ____________________"
1 John 3:4

8. "Therefore by the deeds of the ___________there shall no

flesh be justified in his sight. **Romans 3:20**

9. "Think not that I am come to destroy the _____________, or the

prophets: I am not come to destroy, but to _____________

Matthew 5:17

By this, we know that we love the children of God when we love God and keep His commandments.

1 John 5:3 tells us that "For this is the love of God, that we keep his commandments: and his commandments are not grievous."

1 John 5:5 says, "Who is he that overcometh the world, but he that believeth that Jesus is the Son of God?"

10. If I love Jesus, What will I do? **John 14:15**

____

11. If you keep My _______________________________, you will abide

in My love, just as I have kept My Father's commandments and

abide in His love. **John 15:10**

12. Now by this, we know that we know Him if we keep His

____ **1 John 2:3**

13. For this is the _______________ of God, that _________ keep His

commandments. And His commandments are not burdensome.

1 John 5:3

Summary

1. The 10 commandments were written with the finger of God. **Exodus 31:18**

2. The 10 commandments were put in the ark. **Exodus 25:21-22**

3. The 10 commandments are holy and just and good. **Romans 7:12**

4. Jesus came to fulfill not to destroy the law. **Matthew 5:17**

5. The 10 commandments are not burdensome. **1 John 5:3**

LESSON 7 The Signs of the Times

Purpose: To show biblical evidence of the signs of the times

Objectives: To learn how the signs point to Christ's Second Coming

1. "Now learn a parable of the _______________________;   When his branch is yet tender, and putteth for th leaves, ye know that summer is nigh" **Matthew. 24:32**

2. According to **Luke 21:11**, the three great signs from heaven are

    a. _______________________

    b. _______________________

    c. _______________________

<table>
<tr><td>Note: In scripture, tribulation means the troubles and anxiety, sorrow, or pain which comes from hostility and ill-treatment</td></tr>
</table>

3. After the tribulation, what happens? **Matthew 24:29**

____

____

____

____

____

Matthew 24:12	"And because iniquity shall ______________, the _________________of many shall wax cold."
Mark 13:8	"For nation shall rise against nation, and kingdom against kingdom: and there shall be _________ in diverse places, and there shall be _________and __________: these are the beginnings of sorrows."
Acts 1:11	"Which also said, Ye men of Galilee, why stand ye gazing up into heaven? ___________, which is taken up from you into heaven, shall so _________as ye have seen him go into heaven."

4. When Jesus returns, what happens? **Revelation 1:7**

____

____

____

____

5. Then the sign of the Son of Man will appear in heaven, and

Then all the tribes of the earth will mourn, and they will see the

__________________________________ coming on the clouds of heaven

with ____
   Matthew 24:30

6. When the _____________________________________ comes in His

glory, and all the [a]holy angels with Him, then He will __________ on

the throne of His glory. **Matthew 25:31**

7. Then Jesus said to them, "When you lift up the Son of Man, then you will know that ___________________, and that I do nothing of Myself; but as My Father taught Me, I speak these things **John 8:28**

8. But He kept silent and answered nothing. Again the high priest asked Him, saying to Him, "Are You the ____________, the Son of the Blessed?" Jesus said, "________________. And you will see the Son of Man sitting at the right hand of the Power, and coming with the clouds of heaven." Then the high priest tore his clothes and said, "What further need do we have of witnesses? **Mark 14:61-63**

Note: Jesus is the Son of Man, this is one of His titles

> **Note:** Why is Christ's second coming important to me? Because God keeps His promises; is longsuffering because God doesn't want any person to perish, but that all should come to repentance," Jesus Keeps His promises!
>
> ### Jesus Is The Way, the Truth, and the Life, Follow Him
>
> "Let not your heart be troubled; you believe in God, believe also in Me. 2 In My Father's house are many [a]mansions; if it were not so, [b]I would have told you. I go to prepare a place for you. 3 And if I go and prepare a place for you, I will come again and receive you to Myself; that where I am, there you may be also.

9. What should we do when things begin

(Preparing for Coming of the Son of Man)? **Luke 21:28**

____

____

____

10. For the _________________ Himself will descend from

_________________ with a shout, with the voice of an archangel, and

with the trumpet of God. And the dead in Christ will rise first.

1 Thessalonians 4:16.

11. Why should we be watching for Jesus' return? **Matthew 24:42**

____

____

____

11. Why does Jesus tell us to be ready for His return? **Matthew 25:13**

____

____

____

Jesus Christ Return

Revelation 22:12 And behold, I am coming quickly, and My reward is with Me, to give to every one according to his work.

Hebrews 9:28 so Christ was offered once to bear the sins of many. To those who eagerly wait for Him He will appear   a second time, apart from sin, for salvation.

1 John 2:28 And now, little children, abide in Him, that [a]when He appears, we may have confidence and not be ashamed before Him at His coming.

Revelation 22:20 He who testifies to these things says, "Surely I am coming quickly."

Jesus cautions...

 The disciples had asked the Master concerning the times, when will these **things** be? Christ's answer was more about what was not asked. What shall be the **sign**? The prophecy focuses its attention on the destruction of Jerusalem and then the establishment of Christ's kingdom, judgment, and the last days.

 Jesus cautions us today as He did to His disciples, to stand firm against false teachers. And He warns that there will be wars and problems between m a n y nations, of people being hungry and of illness that have no cure.

LUKE 21:11: "AND great earthquakes shall be in divers places, and famines, and pestilences; and fearful sights and great signs shall there be from heaven."

According to the United States Geological Survey, an average of sixteen earthquakes of magnitude 7 or greater (the size seismologists define as major) have happened worldwide every year since 1900.

Isaiah 51:6 Lift up your eyes to the heavens, And look on the earth beneath. For the heavens will vanish away like smoke,
The earth will grow old like a garment, And those who dwell in it will die in like manner; But My salvation will be forever, And My righteousness will not be abolished.

Magnitude 7.3 or higher **Matthew 24:7, Mark 13:8,** and **Luke 21:11**

Date	Location	Magnitude	Deaths
Jan 28, 2020	Jamaica Jamaica	7.7	0
May 26, 2019	Peru Peru	8	2
Aug 19, 2018	Fiji Fiji	8.2	0
Sept 8, 2017	Mexico Mexico	8.2	98
Dec 17, 2016	Papua New Guinea Papua New Guinea	7.9	0
Aug 24, 2016	ITALY	6.2	600
April 25, 2015	Nepal	7.8	8,000
Sept 16, 2015	Chile Chile	8.3	14
Apr 1, 2014	Chile Chile	8.2	6
Aug. 3, 2014	China	6.2	700
May 24, 2013	Russia Russia	8.3	0
Apr 11, 2012	IndonesiaIndonesia, Indian Ocean	8.6	10
Mar 11, 2011	JapanJapan	9	20,896
Jan 13, 2010	Port-au-Prince	7.0	316,000
Feb 27, 2010	ChileChile	8.8	525

Sings of Jesus Soon Return

What does the Bible say about Earthquakes in diverse places?

Matthew 24:7

For nation shall rise against nation, and kingdom against kingdom: and there shall be famines, and pestilences, and earthquakes, in divers places.

Luke 21:11

And great earthquakes shall be in divers places, and famines, and pestilences; and fearful sights and great signs shall there be from heaven.

At 1:51 p.m., August 23, 2011, a 5.8 magnitude earthquake rattled Virginia.
At 2:15 a.m. on December 16, 1811, a magnitude 7.5 earthquake in northeast Arkansas
At 3:45 a.m., February 7, 1812, a magnitude 7.5 earthquake struck near New Madrid, Missouri

Is there a relationship between and the time of the end? Is this one of the signs of the times Jesus spoke about to the disciples?

Matthew 24:1-7 Then Jesus went out and departed from the temple, and His disciples came up to show Him the buildings of the temple. 2 And Jesus said to them, "Do you not see all these things? Assuredly, I say to you, not one stone shall be left here upon another, that shall not be thrown down."
3 Now as He sat on the Mount of Olives, the disciples came to Him privately, saying, "Tell us, when will these things be? And what will be the sign of Your coming, and of the end of the age?"
4 And Jesus answered and said to them: "Take heed that no one deceives you. 5 For many will come in My name, saying, 'I am the Christ,' and will deceive many. 6 And you will hear of wars and rumors of wars. See that you are not troubled; for [a]all these things must come to pass, but the end is not yet. 7 For nation will rise against nation, and kingdom against

kingdom. And there will be famines, [b]pestilences, and earthquakes in various places.

Summary

1. The sign of the Son of Man will appear in heaven. **Matthew 24:30**

2. For nation shall rise against nation. **Mark 13:8**

3. There will be great earthquakes shall be in divers places. **Luke 21:11**

4. Jesus will appear a second time. **Hebrews 9:28**

5. We should be watching and ready for Jesus' return. **Matthew 24:42, Matthew 25:13**

LESSON 8 The Second Coming of Jesus Christ

Purpose: To provide biblical evidence of Christ's Second Coming

Objectives: To develop knowledge of Christ's Second Coming

To Christ's second coming will occur

1. So Christ was once offered to bear the __of many; and unto them that look for Him shall He ________the second time without sin unto _________ **Hebrews 9:28**.

2. What are 3 things are in Christ's promises?
    John 14: 1-3

    a. _______________________________________

    b. _______________________________________

    c. _______________________________________

3. What words did Christ use in **Luke 24:39** to convince the

disciples t h a t he was physically alive after His death and
resurrection?

____

____

____

4. When the _______________________ comes in His glory, and all

the holy angels with Him, then He will sit on the throne of His

glory **Matthew 25:31**.

5. How was Christ taken to heaven? **Acts 1:9**

____

6. How will Christ return the second time? **Acts 1:11**

____

____

____

6. Who will see Christ when He returns? **Revelation1:7**

____

____

____

7. What should we be looking for? **Titus 2:13**

____

____

____

8. Who knows the day that Jesus will return? **Matthew 24:36**

____

9. What does **Mark 13:27** say is the work of the holy angels during

Christ's second coming?

____

10. Who shall descend from heaven, and how? Who shall arise first?

1 Thessalonians 4:16-17

a. ____

b. ____

c. ____

11. He who testifies to these things says, "Surely I am ________________

quickly. Amen. Even so, come, Lord Jesus! **Revelation 22:20**

12. And if I go and prepare a place for you, I will ________________ again and

receive you to Myself; that where I am, there you may be also. **John 14:3**

13. What will the condition of the world be when Christ returns?
Luke 17:26-27

____

____

____

14. What should we be doing each minute of the day?
Matthew 24:44

____

____

____

THE SECOND COMING OF CHRIST

What is the purpose of Christ's Second Coming?

1. To fulfill His word—**John 14:3**

2. To destroy death—**1 Corinthians 15:25-26**

3. To judge the world—**Matthew 25-46**

4. To reward God's people—**John 3:16**

5. To destroy sin—**Psalms 37:20, 1 Thessalonians 5:3**

What is the manner of Christ's Second Coming?

1. In the clouds—**Matthew 24:30; Revelation 1:7**

2. In flaming fire—**2 Thessalonians 1:7-8,**

3. As a thief—**1 Thessalonians 5:4**

What should we be doing to prepare for Christ's Second Coming?

1. Waiting for the coming of the Lord—**1 Corinthians 1:7**

2. Looking forward to the blessed hope, and the glorious appearing—**Titus 2:13**

3. Watch and be ready—**Matthew 24:42 - 51**

4. Love His appearing—**2 Timothy 4:8**

> **The second coming of Jesus Christ is literal, visible, loud, and definitely not a secret. It is the event of the ages**

Summary

1. We should be looking forward to the blessed hope, and the glorious appearing—**Titus 2:13**

2. Jesus is coming with Angels -- **Revelation1:7**

3. Jesus is coming in the clouds—**Matthew 24:30; Revelation 1:7**

4. Jesus is coming to judge the world—**Matthew 25-46**

5. Jesus is coming and To destroy sin—**Psalms 37:20, 1 Thessalonians 5:3**

LESSON 9 The Day of Judgment

Purpose: To Know God has appointed a Day of Judgment

Objectives: To learn about Judgment

To know who God will judge

> **Note:** Should we be judged? Is there fairness in God's judgment? The word judgment occurs 294 times in 285 different verses in the Bible.
> God is clear about who will judge us and why we are to be judged. Jesus says in **John 5:30** "I can of mine own self do nothing: as I hear I judge: and my judgment is just; because I seek not mine own will, but the will of the Father which hath sent me." We must understand Christ will be our judge.

1. Who has all judgment been placed in the hands? **John 5:22**

____

____

____

2. Who will appear before the judgment seat? **2 Corinthians 5:10**

____

____

____

3. What has come? **Revelation 14:7**

____

____

____

4. Who is the "Ancient of Days?" **Daniel 7:11-13**

____

____

____

5. What does the Bible say about judging one another?
   Romans 14:13

____

____

6. Who will judge the wicked? **Ecclesiastes 3:17**

____

____

7. "Where does judgment begin? **1Peter. 4:17**

____

8. Who was judgment/eternal fire for? **Matthew 25:41**

a. ____________________________

b. ____________________________

c. ____________________________

9. Who will bring every work to judgment? **Ecclesiastes 12:14**

____

____

10. Why did God send His Son into the world? **John 3:17**

____

____

Summary

1. All judgment has been given to the Son.-- **John 5:22**

2. For we must all appear before the judgment seat of Christ.-- **2 Corinthians 5:10**

3. Worship Him who made heaven and earth, the sea and springs of water. **Revelation 14:7**

4. For the time has come for judgment to begin at the house of God--**1 Peter 4:17**

5. God the Father is the Ancient of Days **Daniel 7:11-13**

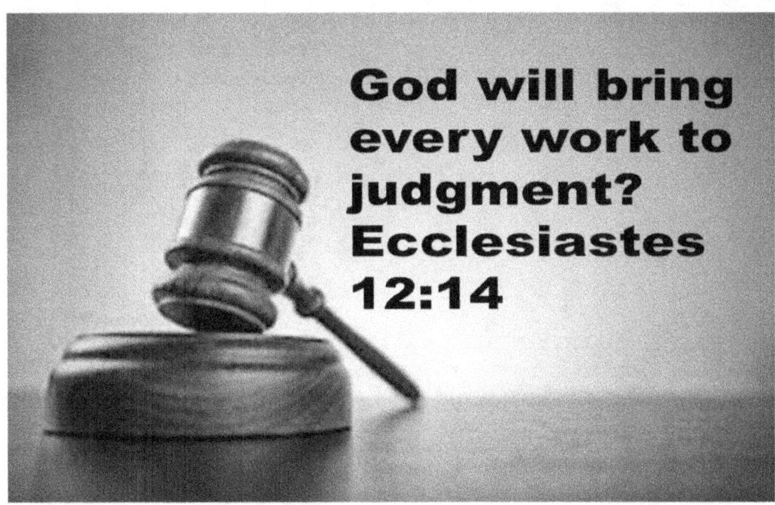

LESSON 10 Tithes and Offerings

Purpose: To learn about tithes and offerings.

Objectives: To learn what God owns.

1. What is our source of getting wealth? **Deuteronomy 8:18**

____

____

2. How much of the tithe belongs to the Lord? **Leviticus 27:30**

____

____

3. How much is the tithe? See **Leviticus 27:32**

____

____

4. Why did the Lord give the children of Levi all the tithes?

Numbers 18:21

____

____

5. What blessing will we receive when we honor the LORD with our first fruits. **Proverbs 3:10**

____

____

> **Note:** Giving shows our of God's love. We cannot out-give God. The truth is that we do not own anything- we are only stewards appointed by God over earthly belongings. I give a tenth of any money that is given to me or earned by me.
>
> **Psalm 24:**1 says, "The earth is the Lord's and the fullness thereof; the world, and they that dwell therein." We are only returning to God a small portion of what He has given us. Like life and breath, God's mercy and grace can never be paid for.

6. "I will surely give the ________________ unto thee"

   Genesis 28:22

7. How can we rob God? **Malachi 3:8**

   ____

   ____

8. What does God do for you when you give back to Him?
Malachi.3:10

____

____

9. You must set aside a ____________of your crops—one-tenth of

all the crops you harvest each year. (MSG) **Deuteronomy 14:22**

10. What is God's expectations of me and tithes? **Luke 16:10-12**

____

11. What should each of us be focused on daily in light of **Matthew 6:33**?

____

12. What does the Lord own? **Psalms 24:1**

____

13. The _________________ is Mine, and the _________________ is

Mine,' says the Lord of hosts **Haggai. 2:8**

14. Based on the Bible, what does a man own? **Haggai 2:8,**

   Psalms 24:1

____

____

15. What shall a man do in exchange for his soul? **Matthew 16:24**

____

____

Summary

1. God gives you the power to get wealth.—
    Deuteronomy 8:18

2. We can rob in tithes and offerings. **Malachi 3:8**

3. When we return tithes and offering our blessings are
    over flowing.-- **Malachi 3:10**

4. The Lord owns everything.-- **Haggai 2:8**

5. Daily I should seek first the kingdom of God and His
    righteousness.-- **Matthew 6:33**

☐**LESSON 11 Temperance**

Purpose: To learn what God says about eating and drinking

Objectives: To know what God desires for us

1. What has God given you for meat? **Genesis1:9:3**

____

____

2. "Therefore, whether you eat or drink, or whatever you do, do all to what? **1 Corinthians 10:31**

____

____

3. "Listen carefully to the Lord, What should I eat? **Isaiah 55:2**

____

____

4. How does the Bible describe you? **Deuteronomy 14:2**

____

____

____

5 "You shall not eat any____________________________

Deuteronomy 14:3

6. "Why is the swine unclean (not to be eaten)? **Leviticus 11:7**

____

7. What does the Bible say about touching the swine? See
Deuteronomy 14:8

____

8. What will be the fate of those eating swine? **Isaiah 66:17**

____

____

____

9. What type of fish are we to eat? **Leviticus 11:12**

____

____

____

10. What two reasons must food from the water/sea/ocean have to be clean? **Deuteronomy 14:9**

____

____

____

11. What four things does God ask of us if we are to avoid the
diseases of the Egyptians? **Exodus 15:26**

A ____

B ____

C ____

D ____

12. "Beloved, now we are ___________________ of God; and it has
not yet been revealed what we shall be, but we know that when He
is revealed, we shall be like Him, for we shall see Him as He is.
1 John 3:2

13. How does the Bible describe your body? **1 Corinthians 6:19**

____

14. How are we to present our bodies before God? **Romans 12:1**

____

15. "What does God say we should be? Why? **Leviticus 11:45**

____

Summary

1. Listen carefully to the Lord, and eat what is good.—
    Isaiah 55:2

2. We are a holy people to the Lord.—
    Deuteronomy 14:2

3. We shall be like Him, for we shall see Him as He is.
    1 John 3:2

4. God has a given us a diet to follow.—
    Deuteronomy 14:3, 9

5. My body is the temple of the Holy Spirit.--
    1 Corinthians 6:19

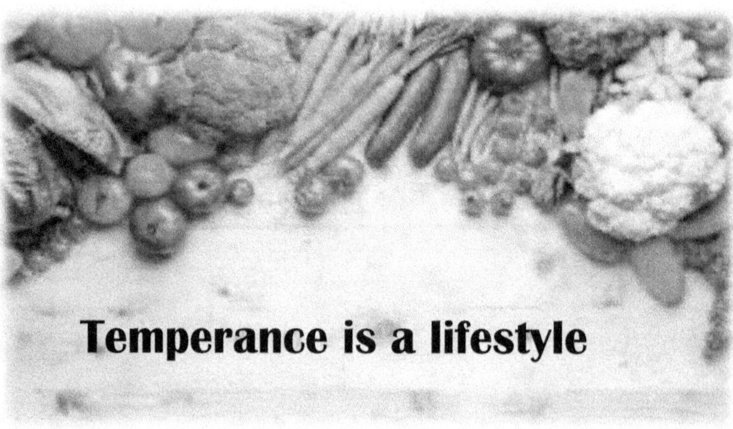

LESSON 12 Where Are the Dead?

Purpose: To learn about what happens when people die

Objectives: To understand what the Bible says about the dead

To understand what makes a living soul.

Food for Thought: If the righteous went to heaven when they died, there would be no need of a resurrection. There could be no reason for Christ to come back to this earth the second time to gather His saints (**John 14:3**) if they had already gone to heaven at death. If the wicked go to hell-fire at death, and the righteous go to heaven at death, there is no need of a judgment day at the end of time, or for Christ to come to reward every person according to His works (**Matthew 16:27; Revelation 22:12**).

What does the Bible say regarding a living soul?

What have many come to accept as biblical truth about the state of the dead?

Why would God take only imperfective dust to heaven?

1. What did God form man from? **Genesis 2:7**

____

2. What element when added to dust creates a living soul?

Genesis 2:7

____

____

3. Solomon says there is a time for everything

A time to be _______________________________________

And a time to _______________________________________

A time to _______________________________________

And a time to _______________________________________

Ecclesiastes 3:2

LIKE ALL GOD'S CREATION, HUMAN BEINGS HAVE A BEGINNING, AN END, AND A PURPOSE.

4. What is clear about the living and the dead?
Ecclesiastes 9:5-6

____

____

____

5. What things would you not find in the grave? **Ecclesiastes 9:10**

A ____

B ____

C ____

6. "For Sheol cannot _________________, Death cannot

_____________; Those who go down to the pit cannot

______________ for Your truth. **Isaiah 38:18**

7. "For in death there is _______________ of thee: in the

_______________ who shall give thee thanks? **Psalms 6:5**

Note: What happens when death occurs? Are we in heaven, hell, or someplace between after death? At death, the body goes back to dust; the spirit returns to God who gave it. This spirit which returns back to God is not some being capable of a conscious existence apart from the body. Rather, it is the breath of life **(James 2:26)**, which God gave to humans to make us living, conscious personalities (**Genesis 2:7**). At death, that life returns to God until the second coming of Christ. That person is asleep in the grave.

8. What happens to people who go down to the grave? **Job 7:9**

____

9. What happens once a man lies down in the grave? **Job 14:12**

____

10. What happens to person's thoughts once they die?

   Psalms 146:4

____

11. The _____________________ do not praise the Lord, Nor any who go down into silence. **Psalms 115:17**

12. What happens to the spirit at death? **Ecclesiastes 12:7**

____

____

____

14. How does the Bible describe Lazarus after he has died? **John 11:11**

____

15. Therefore He says: "Awake, you who _______________, Arise from the dead, And _____________ will give you light. **Ephesians 5:14**

Summary

1. Solomon says there is a time for everything.—**Ecclesiastes 3:2**

2. For the living know that they will die; But the dead know nothing. **Ecclesiastes 9:5-6**

3. When a person dies, they will not awake Nor be roused from their sleep.-- **Job 14:12**

4. The spirit will return to God who gave it. **Ecclesiastes 12:7**

5. The dead are asleep.-- **John 11:11**

LESSON 13   God's Holy Day

Purpose: To understand God's Holy day

Objectives: To learn what the Bible says about the Sabbath

To understand the importance of the Sabbath

1. "What day is the Sabbath of the Lord? **Exodus 20:10**

____

2. What did God tell us not to do on the Sabbath? **Exodus 20:10**

____

3. What did God do on the Sabbath day? **Exodus 20:10-11**

____

____

4. Who made heaven, earth, and the sea? **Exodus 20:10**

____

5. The 4th commandment begins with what word? **Exodus 20:6**

____

6. What does God ask us to do on the Sabbath? **Exodus 20:8**

____

7. Who is Lord of the Sabbath? **Mark 2: 28**

____

8. What was a custom or habit of Jesus? **Luke 4:16**

____

9. Who was the Sabbath made for? **Mark 2: 27**

____

10. How we are to honor the Lord on the Sabbath. **Isaiah 58:13**

____

____

____

____

11. What day of the week did they come to the sepulcher? **Luke 4:1**

____

12. What day took place before the Sabbath? **Luke 23:54**

____

13. What day had past when they returned to the tomb?

Mark 16:1-2

____

Note: In the book of Genesis, we find that God numbered each day of the week. When we look at the Savior on the cross, we see that the last 2 days are identified with names. Why do you think this is? **Daniel 7:23** "And he shall speak great words against the most High, and shall wear out the saints of the most High, and think to change times and laws: and they shall be given into his hand until a time and times and the dividing of time." Notice the clear reference to "change times and laws." What time? What law? The only commandment in God's law that has time is the fourth commandment. As you read the closing chapter of Christ on the cross and His resurrection, we note 2 important things; (1) Christ rested in the tomb on the Sabbath (2) He rose on the first day of the week. What is the lesson here for us today? Note the commandment is not about worship, but about keeping a day holy!

14. When did the Gentiles ask the disciples to preach to them? **Acts 13:42-44**

____

15. Jesus is our example in many ways. Keeping the Sabbath was His custom—not His tradition. If you want to follow Jesus' example would you choose

______ Tradition or Christ ______

How are we to worship God? O come, let us worship and bow down: let us kneel before the LORD our maker" (**Psalms 95:6**).

Does a day really matter? God is the creator. He created everything, including the weekly cycled. In this cycle, He created 7 days, of which only on a name at the time of creation, He named the Sabbath. All the other days were simply numbered, We find, at the time of Jesus, one other name of a day was given a name; the day of preparation which we call "Good Friday." God gave us the Sabbath for two reasons: (1) to commemorate creation (2) as a sign of our salvation. "For in six days, the Lord made the heavens and the earth, the sea, and all that is in them, but He rested on the seventh day. Therefore the Lord blessed the Sabbath day and made it holy" (**Exodus 20:11**). "I gave them my Sabbaths as a sign between us, so they would know that I the Lord made them holy" (**Ezekiel 20:12**).

Who should be worshipped? "For thou shalt worship no other god: for the LORD, whose name is Jealous, is a jealous God" (**Exodus 34:14**).

 "Then saith Jesus unto him, Get thee hence, Satan: for it is written, Thou shalt worship the Lord thy God, and him only shalt thou serve" (**Matthew 4:10**). The Bible teaches that worship is exclusive to God. The Sabbath day has not changed. It remains Saturday as it has always existed. It's not Jewish, The Commandments were given to all; they are a reflection of God's character.

Summary

1. The Sabbath of the Lord is the 7th day.-- **Exodus 20:10**

2. God asks us to keep the Sabbath holy.-- **Exodus 20:8**

3. Sabbath made for man.-- **Mark 2: 27**

4. Honor God, not doing your own ways.-- **Isaiah 58:13**

5. The disciples to preach to them? **Acts 13:42-44**

LESSON 14 Baptism

Purpose: To understand baptism

Objectives: To know the prerequisites to baptism

To understand why we need to be born again

To learn about the example of Jesus

Note: What is baptism? Does God require it?

Mark 1:4 says, John did baptize in the wilderness, and preach the baptism of repentance for the remission of sins." **Romans 6:4** says, "Therefore we are buried with him by baptism into death: that like as Christ was raised up from the dead by the glory of the Father, even so we also should walk in newness of life."

---

1. What was John the Baptist, preaching in the wilderness of Judaea? **Matthew. 3:1, 2**

____

____

2. What was John the Baptist, preaching about? **Matthew. 3: 2**

____

3. Why was John the Baptist, preaching this message?

   Matthew 3: 2

____

4. What 2 things are we to do to be saved? **Mark 16:16**

____

5. "Who was baptized in Jordan? **Mark 1:9**

____

6. "Whose footsteps should I follow? **1 Peter 2:21**

____

7. Or do you not know that as many of us as were _______________
into Christ Jesus were baptized into His death? **Romans 6:3-4**

8. What happens to those who [a]gladly received His baptismal?

   Acts 2:41

____

9. How many were baptized? **Acts 2:41**

____

10. Jesus says a man be born of what 2 things? **John 3:5**

____

11. Why did Jesus say a man be born of these things? **John 3:5**

____

____

12. What did Philip do to for eunuch? **Acts 8:38**

____

13. Whose name are we to make disciples in? **Matthew 28:19**

____

14. When you are baptized what do you put on? **Galatians 3:27**

____

15. ____________, ____________, ____________ **Ephesians 4:5**

16. What are the Prerequisites to baptism?

a. _______________________________________

____

____

Hebrews 11:1, Hebrews 1:6

b. _______________________________________

____

____

Luke 5:32, Psalms 38:18

c. _______________________________________

____

____

John 20:31

Summary

1. Repent, for the kingdom of heaven is at hand. – **Matthew 3:2**

2. Believe that Jesus is the Christ. -- **John 20:31**

3. We must be born of water and the Spirit.-- **John 3:5**

4. We are baptized into Christ then we put on Christ.— **Galatians 3:27**

5. Baptized in the name of the Father and of the Son and of the Holy Spirit. -- **Matthew 28:19**

LESSON 15 God's True Church

Purpose: To understand that God has a true church

Objectives: To identify the characteristics of God's church

To know Jesus is the head of the church

What is a <u>remnant</u>? What does remnant have to do with God or a church?

The church (Sanctuary/Temple) is the house of God; He dwells there. The church holds forth the Scripture and the doctrine of Christ as a pillar holds up a structure. The church must always be the pillar and ground of truth.

1. How is the house of God described? **1Timothy 3:15**

____

____

2. "The remnant of Israel shall not do what? **Zephaniah 3:13**

____

____

3. What does Christ warn us against? **Colossians 2:8**

____

____

4. If they do not speak according to this word, it is because they don't have what? **Isaiah.8:20**

____

____

5. Who is the light of the world? **John 8:1**

____

____

6. How does Jesus describe Himself? **John 14:6**

____

____

7. Who do true worshipers worship? **John 4:23**

____

____

8. How is He worshiped? **John 4:23**

____

____

9. What did Jesus make clear to us? **Matthew 5:17**

____

____

10. How should we call upon the Lord? **Psalm 145:18**

____

____

11. How does the Bible describe the patience of the saints?
Revelation 14:12

____

____

> **The word, testimony** (Greek in origin) comes from
> the root word marturia, which in its various forms
> means "testifying," "testimony," "witness," and
> "martyr." In relationship to Jesus, it can be understood
> in two ways: (1) the testimony came from Jesus. This
> identifies Jesus as the source of the testimony. (2) The
> testimony is about Jesus. This identifies Jesus is the
> subject of the testimony. The testimony of Jesus Christ
> means receiving personal spiritual assurance through
> the Holy Ghost. The church will be a church that has
> the "testimony of Jesus." The true church will have the
> "testimony of Jesus," which is the Spirit of Prophecy.

12. Who did the dragon go to make war with? **Revelation 12:17**

____

____

13. What did the seed of the woman have? **Revelation 12:17**

____

____

14. The true church will be a church that does the following:

Ephesians 1:22

____

____

Summary

1. The house of God is the church of the living God. --
    1 **Timothy 3:15**

2. The remnant of Israel shall do no unrighteousness. –
    Zephaniah 3:13

3. The true worshipers will worship the Father in spirit
    and truth. **John 4:23**

4.   And the dragon was angry with the woman, and he
went to make war with the rest of her offspring, who keep
the commandments of God and have the testimony of Jesus
Christ. **Revelation 12:17**

5. All things under Jesus' feet. -- **Ephesians 1:22**

Scripture Index

THE HOLY BIBLE: TRUE OR FALSE

John 1:1
2 Timothy 3:15
2 Peter 1:21
Romans 15:4
Isaiah 28:10

2 Timothy 3:16
2 Peter 1:20
John 8:12
2 Timothy 2:15
Psalms 119:105
Matthew 4:4

THE HOLY SPIRIT

Genesis 1:2
Job 33:4
2 Corinthians 13:14
John 16:13
John 14:26
1 Corinthians 12:3
1Corinthians 12:11
Romans 15:30
Genesis 2:7
Leviticus 8:10-12
Ephesians 1:13
John 7:37-39

Psalms 104:30
Matthew 28:19
Acts 5:3-4
Matthew 11:27
1 Corinthians 3:16
Romans 8:27
1Corinthians 2:11
Psalms 143:10
Psalms 51:11
Mathew 3:16
Exodus 3:2

BASIC INSTRUCTIONS BEFORE LEAVING EARTH

2 Timothy 3:17
Hebrew 4:12
Jeremiah 31:3
1 Kings 8:61
John 14:2-3
Ephesians 6:17

2 Timothy 3:16
Psalms 138:2
Psalms 84:11
1 John 2:25
Ephesians 6:11
1 Thessalonians 5:17

WHY STUDY THE BIBLE?

Romans 15:4
Deuteronomy 4:2
Psalms 86:15
John 16:13
Job 12:13
Genesis 1:1
John 3:16
1 John 3:8

2Timothy 2:15
Psalms 86:11
John 16:13
1John 3:8
Matthew 4:4
John 4:7
Psalms 33:9
Philippians 4:13

WHAT IS SIN?

1 John 3:4
Jeremiah 30:12
Proverbs 14:34
Ezekiel 28:15
Proverbs 24:9
James 4:17
1 John 1:7
John 8:12

Matt 7:2
Psalms 51:5
Revelation 12:9
Romans 3:20
Romans 5:12
Romans 3:23
1 Thessalonians 5:9

GOD'S TEN COMMANDMENTS

Exodus 31:18
Psalms 19:7
John 14:15
Romans 7:12
Romans 3:20
John 15:10
1 John 2:3

Exodus. 40:20
Psalms 19:8
Psalms 111:7-8
Job 33:9
Matthew 5:17
1 John 3:4
1 John 3:4

THE SIGNS OF THE TIMES

Matthew 24:32
Matthew 24:31
Matthew 24:7
Matthew 24:12
Acts 1:11
Matthew 24:30
Revelation 5:11
1 Thessalonians 4:16
Matthew 25:13

Matthew 24:29
Luke 21:11
Mark 14:61-63
Mark 13:8
Revelation 1:7
Matthew 25:31
Luke 21:28
Matthew 24:42
Matthew 24:44

Scripture Index

THE SECOND COMING OF CHRIST

Hebrews 9:28
Luke 24:39
Acts 1:11
Matthew 25:31
Mark 13:27
Revelation 22:20
Luke 17:26-27
John 14:1-3
Acts 1:9
Revelation 1:7
Matthew 24:36
1 Thessalonians 4:16-17
Titus 2:13
Matthew 24:44

TITHES AND OFFERINGS

Psalms 24:1
Leviticus 27:30
Numbers 18:21
Genesis 28:22
Malachi 3:10
Luke 16:10-12
Psalms 24:1
Matthew 16:24
Deuteronomy 8:18
Leviticus 27:32
Proverbs 3:10
Malachi 3:8
Deuteronomy 14:22
Matthew 6:33
Haggai 2:8

WHERE ARE THE DEAD?

Genesis 2:7
Ecclesiastes 9:5-6
Isaiah 38:18-19
Job 7:9
Psalms 146:4
Ecclesiastes 12:7
Ecclesiastes 3:2
Ecclesiastes 9:10
John 11:11
Job 14:12
Psalms 115:17
Ecclesiastes 8:8

BAPTISM

Matthew 3:2
Mark 1:9
Romans 6:3-4
Acts 2:41
Acts 8:38
Acts 22:16
Matthew 28:19
Hebrews 1:6
Psalms 38:18
Mark 16:16
1 Peter 2:21
Matthew 3:1-2
John 3:5
Ephesians 4:5
Galatians 3:27
Hebrews 11:1
Luke 5:32
John 20:31

THE DAY OF JUDGMENT

John 5:22
Revelation 14:7
Ecclesiastes 3:17
Matthew 25:4
Romans 14:12
2 Corinthians 5:10
Daniel 7:11-13
1Peter 4:17
John3:17
Ecclesiastes 12:14

TEMPERANCE

Genesis 1: 29
Isaiah 55:2
Leviticus 11:7
Deuteronomy 14:8
Leviticus 11:12
Exodus 15:26
Habakkuk 2:15
1 Corinthians 6:19
1 Corinthians. 10:31
Deuteronomy 14:2
Leviticus 11:45
Isaiah 66:17
Deuteronomy 14:9
Romans 12:2
1 John 3:2
Deuteronomy 14:

GOD'S HOLY DAY

Exodus 20:10
Mark 2: 28
Luke 4:1
Luke 24:1
Acts 13:42-44
Exodus 20:10
Exodus 20:11
Matthew 4:10
Exdous34:14
Luke 4:16
Isaiah 58:13
Mark 16:1-2
Luke 4:14-16
Mark 2:27
Exodus 34:14
Exodus: 20:6
Psalms 95:6
Ezekiel 20:12

GOD'S HOLY CHURCH

1 Timothy 3:15
Zephaniah 3:13
Colossians 2:8
John 4:23
Mathew 5:17
John 8:1
Revelation 12:17
John 14:6
Isaiah 8:20
Psalms 145:18
Revelation 14:12
Ephesians 1:22

```
T H H S S G C G X F V K L R F
H S T S O H N E N I W S A H Y
C I E E M I E I X I O N M C E
H W L N S R V O Z U V A P A V
E B L S Y S A T L I B I R E A
R E E U C L E A N O T T L T R
U L W O R E H R M E H P I L G
B O D E E G E I G U M Y A M V
I V A T M N N T W S R G L B E
M E E H T A B B A S N E D O Q
H D R G T H G I L E Z A T U H
T O B I E C L S N A M O R A J
A L O R D R E F F O C S R T W
E N O I T A V L A S P I R I T
D E K C I W I A T D B C X A V
```

ABOMINATION	ARCHANGEL	BAPTIZING
BELOVED	BLESSING	BREAD
CHERUBIM	CLEAN	DEATH
DWELLETH	EARTH	EGYPTIANS
GRAVE	HEAVEN	HOLY
HOSTS	JUDGMENT	LAMP
LAW	LEVI	LIGHT
LIVING	LORD	MEAT
MERCY	RIGHTEOUSNESS	ROMANS
SABBATH	SALVATION	SCOFFER
SEA	SHEOL	SIN
SOUL	SPIRIT	SWINE
TEACH	TIME	TRANSGRESSETH
WATER	WICKED	

FOUNDATIONAL BIBLE STUDY QUESTION SHEET

1. ____

____

____

2. ____

____

____

3. ____

____

____

4. ____

____

____

5. ____

____

____

6.

7.

8.

9.

10.

<u>2 Timothy 2:15</u> **Study** to shew thyself approved unto God, a workman that needeth not to be ashamed, rightly dividing **the word** of truth.